CASSOWARY

BY CONNOR STRATTON

Apex is distributed by North Star Editions:
sales@northstareditions.com | 888-417-0195

Produced for Apex by Red Line Editorial.

Photographs ©: Shutterstock Images, cover, 1, 4–5, 6, 8–9, 10–11, 13, 14–15, 16–17, 18, 19, 20, 21, 22–23, 26, 29; iStockphoto, 7, 12, 24–25

Library of Congress Control Number: 2022901423

ISBN
978-1-63738-282-0 (hardcover)
978-1-63738-318-6 (paperback)
978-1-63738-389-6 (ebook pdf)
978-1-63738-354-4 (hosted ebook)

Printed in the United States of America
Mankato, MN
082022

NOTE TO PARENTS AND EDUCATORS

Apex books are designed to build literacy skills in striving readers. Exciting, high-interest content attracts and holds readers' attention. The text is carefully leveled to allow students to achieve success quickly. Additional features, such as bolded glossary words for difficult terms, help build comprehension.

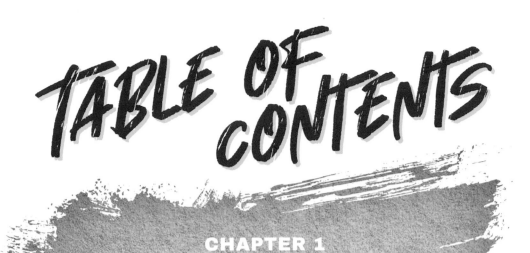

TABLE OF CONTENTS

CHAPTER 1

SHARP KICK

A cassowary walks with its chicks. Their heads bob as their long legs move. Suddenly, they spot a group of dingoes. The dingoes charge.

Cassowary chicks have brown and tan feathers. They change colors when they grow up.

FAST FACT

A cassowary can kick hard enough to break bones.

A cassowary's claws can be up to 4 inches (10 cm) long.

The cassowary must defend its young. It kicks one of the dingoes. It uses the claw on its toe. The claw slashes the dingo. The dingo's body bleeds.

 Dingoes are wild dogs. They often hunt and eat young cassowaries.

A male cassowary guards its chicks and shows them how to find food.

The hurt dingo falls to the ground. The other wild dogs run away. The cassowary's chicks are safe.

DEADLY BUT SHY

Cassowaries are some of Earth's most dangerous birds. However, they rarely attack. Cassowaries are shy. They tend to stay hidden. They kick only if they feel threatened.

CHAPTER 2

LIFE IN THE WILD

Cassowaries are **native** to only a few places. Many are found in Australia. Some also live in New Guinea. Others live on islands nearby.

The name *cassowary* comes from two Papuan words that mean "horned" and "head."

A cassowary's thick feathers look sort of like fur.

Many cassowaries are found in rain forests. But some live in low, swampy areas.

Cassowaries are good swimmers. They sometimes live near coasts or rivers.

Cassowaries cannot fly. Instead, their feathers protect their bodies. They help block rain and sharp plants.

Cassowaries tend to live alone. Males and females come together to **mate**. The females lay eggs. Then they leave. The males sit on the eggs. They raise the babies, too.

A male cassowary sits on eggs for about 50 days before they hatch.

GROWING UP

Cassowaries usually lay three to six eggs at a time. After chicks hatch, they stay with the male cassowary for about 10 months. Then he chases them away. The young birds go to live on their own.

CHAPTER 3

ODD BIRDS

Cassowaries are large birds. Some grow to be 6 feet (2 m) tall. Cassowaries are very fast. They can run up to 31 miles per hour (50 km/h).

Some adult cassowaries can jump 7 feet (2.1 m) off the ground.

Every cassowary has a casque. This body part is like a helmet. It sticks out from the bird's head.

FAST FACT

Cassowaries aren't born with casques. The casques grow after a year or two.

Female cassowaries tend to have larger casques than males do.

Dwarf cassowaries are the smallest type. Most are 40 to 50 inches (102–127 cm) tall.

There are three types of cassowaries. The southern cassowary is the largest. Two wattles hang from its neck. The northern cassowary has only one wattle. The dwarf cassowary has none.

BIRD BOOMS

Cassowaries communicate with booms. Booms are very low sounds. People almost can't hear them. But people can feel the booms in their bodies.

A southern cassowary's wattles are bright red.

CHAPTER 4

FRUIT LOVERS

Cassowaries eat mostly fruit. They eat fruit from more than 200 different plants. They eat some seeds and **fungi**, too.

Cassowaries may eat more than 10 pounds (4.5 kg) of fruit in one day.

Cassowaries spend about one-third of their time looking for food.

Cassowaries look for food at dawn and dusk. They find fruits that have dropped to the forest floor. Their claws help them pick through fallen leaves.

SEED SPREADER

Cassowaries don't digest seeds well. As a result, plants can sprout from their droppings. By spreading seeds, cassowaries help rain forests stay healthy. They help many types of trees grow.

FAST FACT

Sometimes cassowaries eat poop. The poop still has bits of fruit in it.

Cassowaries sometimes eat small animals. But they don't usually hunt. They don't usually hurt people, either. In fact, people are a bigger danger to the birds.

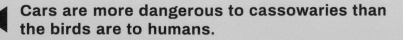

Cars are more dangerous to cassowaries than the birds are to humans.

COMPREHENSION QUESTIONS

Write your answers on a separate piece of paper.

1. Write a sentence describing how cassowaries look for food.

2. Would you want to see a cassowary in real life? Why or why not?

3. Which type of cassowary is the largest?

    A. dwarf cassowary

    B. northern cassowary

    C. southern cassowary

4. What might happen to rain forests if cassowaries disappeared?

    A. More types of plants would grow.

    B. Fewer plants would grow.

    C. Nothing would change.

5. What does slashes mean in this book?

The claw slashes the dingo. The dingo's body bleeds.

    A. blocks

    B. closes up

    C. cuts open

6. What does protect mean in this book?

Instead, their feathers protect their bodies. They help block rain and sharp plants.

    A. keep safe

    B. cause harm

    C. change shape

Answer key on page 32.

GLOSSARY

charge
To run at something, often for an attack.

communicate
To send and receive messages.

digest
To break down food so the body can get energy from it.

fungi
Living things, such as mushrooms, that break stuff down.

mate
To form a pair and come together to have babies.

native
Originally living in an area.

sprout
To begin to grow.

threatened
Put in danger.

wattles
Fleshy body parts that hang from the necks of certain birds. Turkeys, roosters, and cassowaries all have wattles.

TO LEARN MORE

BOOKS

Harvey, Derek. *Nature's Deadliest Creatures*. London: DK Children, 2018.

Levy, Janey. *Cassowary vs. Rhinoceros*. New York: Gareth Stevens Publishing, 2021.

Mattern, Joanne. *Most Dangerous*. South Egremont, MA: Red Chair Press, 2020.

ONLINE RESOURCES

Visit www.apexeditions.com to find links and resources related to this title.

ABOUT THE AUTHOR

Connor Stratton writes and edits nonfiction children's books. He is grateful to have never encountered any of the world's deadliest animals.

INDEX

ANSWER KEY:
1. Answers will vary; 2. Answers will vary; 3. C; 4. B; 5. C; 6. A